BRIGHT IDEA BOOKS

HOW DO Cars DRIVE THEMSELVES?

by Marcia Amidon Lusted

Content Consultant

Jeffrey Miller, Ph.D.
University of Southern California

CAPSTONE PRESS
a capstone imprint

Bright Idea Books are published by Capstone Press
1710 Roe Crest Drive, North Mankato, Minnesota 56003
www.mycapstone.com

Library of Congress Cataloging-in-Publication Data
Names: Lusted, Marcia Amidon, author.
Title: How do cars drive themselves? / by Marcia Amidon Lusted.
Description: North Mankato, Minnesota : Capstone Press, [2019] | Series:
   How'd they do that? | "Bright Idea Books are published by Capstone Press."
   | Audience: Grades 4 to 6. | Includes bibliographical references and index.
Identifiers: LCCN 2018018709 (print) | LCCN 2018024814 (ebook) | ISBN
   9781543541809 (ebook) | ISBN 9781543541403 (hardcover : alk. paper)
Subjects: LCSH: Autonomous vehicles--Juvenile literature. |
   Automobiles--Automatic control--Juvenile literature. | Automobiles--Design
   and construction--Juvenile literature. | Automobile industry and
   trade--Technological innovations--Juvenile literature.
Classification: LCC TL152.8 (ebook) | LCC TL152.8 .L87 2019 (print) | DDC 629.22--dc23
LC record available at https://lccn.loc.gov/2018018709

Editorial Credits
Editor: Megan Gunderson
Designer: Becky Daum
Production Specialist: Colleen McLaren

Photo Credits
AP Images: Bei Piao/Imaginechina, 18–19, Jose Juarez/Detroit News, cover (foreground), Philip Toscano/Press Association/URN: 30544691, 16–17, Uli Deck/picture-alliance/dpa, 11; Getty Images: Visual China Group, 5; iStockphoto: Chesky_W, 24–25, JasonDoiy, 14–15, 20–21, 28, 30–31, metamorworks, 22–23, zenstock, 6–7; Shutterstock Images: Grzegorz Czapski, 26, hxdyl, cover (background), metamorworks, 8–9, 13

Design Elements: iStockphoto, Red Line Editorial, and Shutterstock Images

TABLE OF CONTENTS

CHAPTER 1

WHO'S Driving?

A car moves through city streets. It pauses for people crossing. It waits for a green light. Then it neatly parks near a store.

Later the car heads to the freeway. It merges smoothly with other cars. What is so unusual? No one is driving it!

Self-driving cars don't need human drivers. They steer themselves. Self-driving cars are real. Someday they will be a common sight.

Self-driving cars hit the road!

ON THE WAY

Already some cars are partly self-driving. Many cars have cruise control. This keeps the car at a set speed.

Others have special braking systems. They use **sensors** in the front. The sensors see when another car is too close.

If the system thinks there might be a crash, it uses the brakes. The car slows. It avoids a crash.

CRUISE

RES
+

CANCEL

−
SET

Cruise control keeps a car's speed steady without the driver's help.

In the future, a driver could decide whether to let the car drive itself.

No car yet is fully self-driving.
Engineers are working on cars that
mostly drive themselves. The cars do
most of the work. But they still need
drivers to make some decisions.

Can we replace a human driver completely? Engineers are working hard to make this happen. Soon these cars of the future will be on the streets.

COMING SOON

Some companies are already designing self-driving cars. These include Tesla, Mercedes, BMW, and Audi. Tech companies like Google and Uber are too.

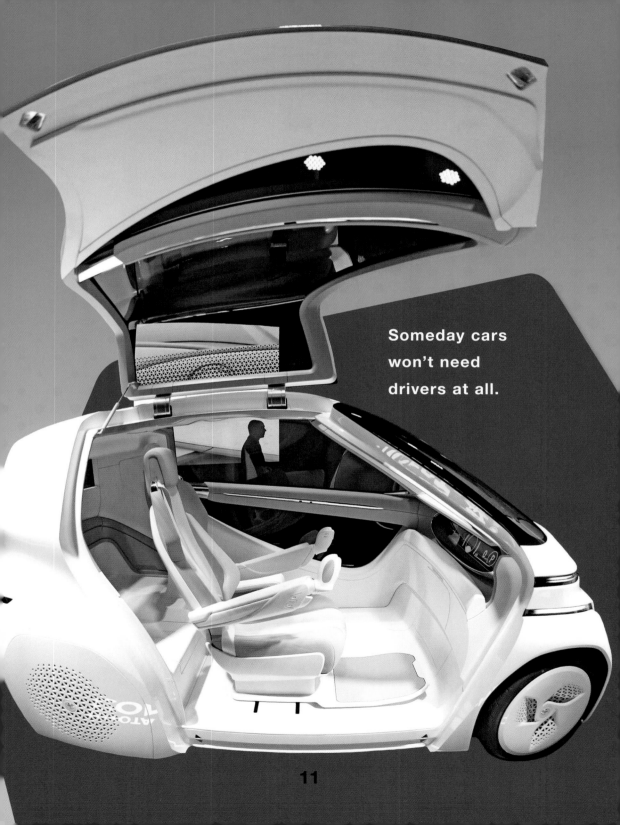

Someday cars won't need drivers at all.

11

CHAPTER 2

HOW IS IT Driving?

How can engineers make a car drive itself? Computer systems must replace the driver. They must work together to drive the car.

LOOK OUT AHEAD

A driver must look out for objects ahead. A driverless car must do the same. Its sensors act as its eyes.

A self-driving car needs to sense everything around it.

These cars sense their surroundings with **lidar**. The lidar system looks like a bubble. It spins all the time.

Lidar uses lasers and scanners. Lasers bounce off nearby things. The system senses everything around the car. This way, the car avoids anything in its way.

Lidar usually sits
on top of the car.

15

Self-driving cars also use **radar**. Radar uses radio waves. The waves bounce off objects. Computers measure the waves. They map the car's surroundings.

ARE WE THERE YET?

The car needs to know where it is. It also needs to know where to go. Computers store the car's maps. Some maps show where the car is going. Other maps show what is around the car.

The car also uses **GPS.** The GPS network has satellites. The car uses the network to know where it is.

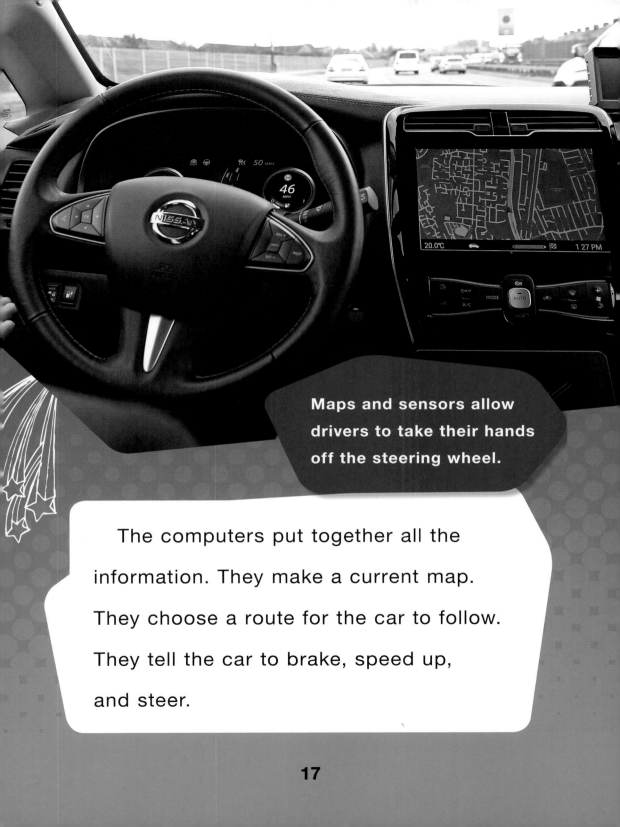

Maps and sensors allow drivers to take their hands off the steering wheel.

The computers put together all the information. They make a current map. They choose a route for the car to follow. They tell the car to brake, speed up, and steer.

A car must be programmed to follow traffic laws.

IT'S THE LAW

The car also must follow traffic laws. The car's computers know the speed limits. They note special traffic conditions.

More important, the car must make decisions. Another car might run a red light. How will the self-driving car react? It must track the situation. It must decide when to brake.

WHERE'S THE STEERING WHEEL?

Totally self-driving cars will look different! The car will not need a steering wheel. It will not even need pedals on the floor.

CHAPTER 3

WHY GO
Driverless?

Why do we need self-driving cars? Today there are many problems with driving. People think these cars can help solve the problems.

There is still much to do before self-driving cars are safe and common.

STAY SAFE

Thousands of people die in traffic accidents every year. Self-driving cars will be safer than traditional cars.

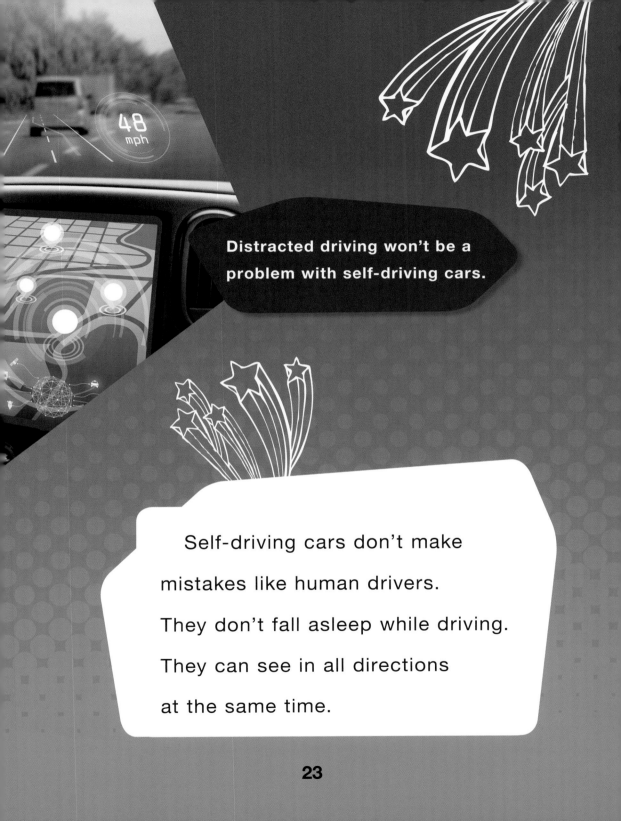

Distracted driving won't be a problem with self-driving cars.

Self-driving cars don't make mistakes like human drivers. They don't fall asleep while driving. They can see in all directions at the same time.

LET ME DRIVE YOU

Some people cannot drive. Self-driving cars will help.

These cars will make it easier for people with **disabilities** to travel. Kids will not need a parent to drive them.

In a self-driving car, a driver could turn around to face the passengers.

SHARE THE ROAD

Self-driving cars can cut down on **pollution**. Many of these cars will be electric. They will harm Earth less.

Fewer cars would also help the planet. Some people hope self-driving cars will be shared more. Then there will be fewer cars on the road.

THE FUTURE

Self-driving cars are the cars of the future! They will be safer. They will help everyone get around. And they could be good for Earth. Those are very important reasons for designing and building them.

WE NEED YOU

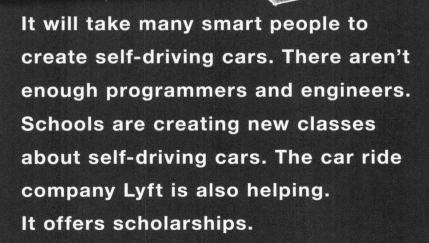

It will take many smart people to create self-driving cars. There aren't enough programmers and engineers. Schools are creating new classes about self-driving cars. The car ride company Lyft is also helping. It offers scholarships.

GLOSSARY

disability
a physical or mental condition that limits a person's ability to do various tasks

engineer
a person who designs, builds, and fixes machines

GPS
Global Positioning System, a system of satellites that can determine the position of a person or vehicle

lidar
a sensing system that uses light from a laser

pollution
substances that make land, water, or air dirty, unsafe, or unusable

radar
a sensing system that uses radio waves

sensor
a device that measures and responds to inputs like heat, motion, moisture, or other conditions

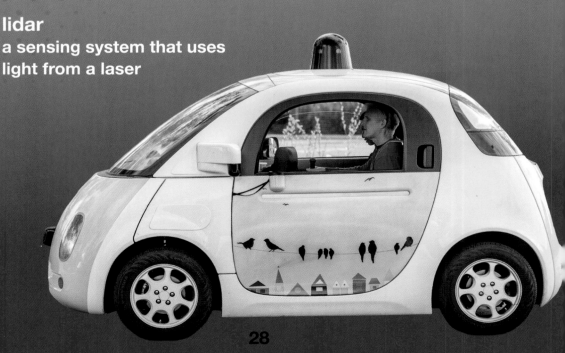

TRIVIA

1. Robotic taxis: The Nissan car company is testing self-driving taxis in Japan. These taxis will drive on preset routes. Passengers can use a phone app to call the taxi and pay for it.

2. Self-driving trucks: Self-driving trucks are already being tested. Trucks usually drive long, straight roads. There are few twists and turns. These routes are easier for self-driving trucks.

3. Flying cars? The Uber ridesharing company is testing flying cars. They will be similar to helicopters and drones. They will take off and land from rooftops. The cars are only for short trips, usually in cities. Eventually these cars will be self-driving.

ACTIVITY

Imagine you are an engineer. Design a car that drives itself. What special features does it have? How is it different from traditional cars?

Choose a place where you'd like the car to go. Draw a simple map from your home or school to that place.

Write a list of instructions for your driverless car based on your map. What does it have to do first? Which ways will it have to turn? When will it have to slow down or speed up? What does it have to look for, such as street signs or walkers? Make the list as complete as you can. Read your finished list out loud to a friend. Do the steps make sense to your friend? Have you left out anything?

EXTRA:

If you or your classroom have a robotics system that lets you build vehicles and program them (such as Lego Mindstorms), try programming your car to drive itself over your map.

FURTHER RESOURCES

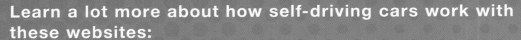

Learn a lot more about how self-driving cars work with these websites:

How Driverless Cars Will Work
https://auto.howstuffworks.com/under-the-hood/trends-innovations/
    driverless-car.htm

The Race for Self-Driving Cars
https://www.nytimes.com/interactive/2016/12/14/technology/
    how-self-driving-cars-work.html

Read about the future for self-driving cars in these books:

Marsico, Katie. *Self-Driving Cars.* New York: Children's Press, 2016.

Newman, Lauren. *Self-Driving Cars.* Ann Arbor, Mich.: Cherry Lake
    Publishing, 2018.

INDEX